Acknowledgements

This book began with a simple prompt by my dear friend, colleague and business strategist Maresa Freidman, CEO of The Executive Cat Herder. Maresa asked me to write 52 ideas about resilience – that was the easy part! Of course, she then asked me to write a paragraph or two about each idea. And months later here it is! Thank you Maresa for being a constant source of inspiration to me

Well of course the book wasn't that easy, first I had to have enough life challenges over the years to get my attention and cause me to live in resilience. Then I called my virtual assistant Charlie! I can honestly say that this book would not have come to fruition without her help. It is from the bottom of my heart that I thank you for your love, support and project management Charlotte Constantin! Then there were the interns from the University of California San Diego (UCSD). Many thanks to Larry Destro for securing not one, not two, but THREE interns to assist with this project: Nicolas Vincent, Theo Fuller, Bastien Ugolini, thank you for researching book covers, quotes and statistics on resilience.

Every day I am inspired and thankful for the support and encouragement of my family. Vey Linville is the most supportive person I have ever had in my life. He lifts me up when my spirits are down and believes in me even when I don't believe in myself. Thanks for your fine eye for edits my dear! My children Shane, Danielle and Rachel have been my reason to persevere. I am blessed to have colleagues who are also dear friends, a few of which visited with me as I was in final edits for the book. Thank you Howard Prager for great recommendations on photo selections, and thanks to Sharon Wingron, Cindy Huggett and Elaine Biech for validating the concept and direction of the book.

It is my tribe of supporters that inspire me to even better than I believe I can be.
Thank you all for believing in me.

Table Of Contents

Acknowledgements	1
Introduction	4
Praise for " A Year of Resilience"	5
1. Find your center	7
2. Be truly present with others	9
3. Take time to enjoy the little things in life	11
4. Be mindful of your health	13
5. Reflect	15
6. Develop new skills	17
7. Develop positive habits	19
8. Find joy every day	21
9. Apply yourself	23
10. Work hard	25
11. Follow your instincts	27
12. Know when it's time to quit	29
13. Seek out kindred spirits	31
14. Explore new places	33
15. Be open to different opinions	35
16. Embrace your loved ones	37
17. Thank the people who support you	39
18. Be there for others	41
19. Give back	43
20. Practice mindfulness	45
21. Breathe	47
22. Stretch Yourself	49

23. Relax 51

24. Connect 53

25. Develop yourself 55

26. Be willing to change 57

27. Allow others to be who they are 59

28. Look past the obstacles 61

29. Collaborate for synergy 63

30. Leverage your resources 65

31. Build bridges - not walls 67

32. Add value 69

33. Embrace the micro moments of balance 71

34. Reframe negative situations 73

35. Pay attention to perspective 75

36. Listen first 77

37. Don't judge others immediately 79

38. Savor the beauty of your surroundings 81

39. Welcome adversity 83

40. Conquer your fears 85

41. Clarify your vision 87

42. Tackle big goals 89

43. Get healthy 91

44. Find your tribe 93

45. Be purposeful 95

46. Prepare 97

47. Know your options 99

48. Choose wisely 101

49. Be true to yourself 103

50. Find your voice 105

51. Speak your truth 107

52. Be courageous 109

Introduction

When I started writing this book I had no idea how much I would be living in resilience – AGAIN! At the end of 2019 I lost the largest long-term contract my business ever had. This contract represented over 80% of my annual revenue, and of course has significant impact on both myself and my team.

The ideas I share in this book I have lived. In fact, I must admit that the old saying from Aesops Fables (circa 560 BC) comes to mind… Be careful what you wish for, lest it come true! Did I bring this on myself by writing about resilience? Who knows? People are not born resilient. Although some individuals seem to readily bounce back from tough situations, others do not. Resilience is a choice to have a positive mindset in spite of the challenges that you face. It's a choice to be purposeful in your behaviors daily to help you strengthen the muscle of resilience.

Resilience is not automatic; it takes concerted effort! This book is formatted simply with an image, a quote and a paragraph or two about each idea for building resilience. I hope you gain some insights that will help you to be more resilient and stay afloat!

My ambition is that this book provides you with insights that will help you to be more resilient and stay afloat!

Praise for *A Year of Resilience*

The ability to bounce back from adversity or failure is a skill we can all learn—and this book shows you how. Resilience isn't about zipping through life unscathed or about how to avoid everyday challenges. No, quite the opposite; it's about experiencing life's natural obstacles to their fullest, learning from them, and continuing to live a joyful, positive life. Maureen Orey has created a practical guide to lead you through your own personal resiliency retreat. The 52 ideas suggest one for each week of the year, but they are so enticing you won't want to stop reading! She presents the importance of being present, giving to others, reflecting on your actions and many others. A Year of Resilience is sure to provide you with the encouragement and capacity you need for a more fulfilled, purposeful, and relaxing year—for your entire life. Don't miss this one!

Elaine Biech, author The Washington Post #1 Best Seller nonfiction: ***The Art and Science of Training*** and ***The New Business of Consulting***

No one can find inner peace except by working,

not in a self- centered way, but for the whole human family.

– Peace Pilgrim

1. Find your center

Resilience requires a sense of balance. Take the time to focus on your strengths while acknowledging any areas of potential development. By knowing your comfort zone and the aspects of your life and work that provide you with feelings of security and fulfillment, you'll be better equipped to stay grounded to leverage your inner strength when times get tough.

Your center is the place of purpose and inner peace that you can go to when life gets ahead of you. It's the head-space you build to keep yourself grounded in times of stress and external pressure or chaos. Some of us find stability and reassurance in professional productivity, while others find their center in social spaces, self-care, meditation, or physical intimacy. There's no right or wrong way to recenter yourself; find the spaces and energies that are restorative for you, then find a way to integrate them into your daily routine. Self-care looks different for everyone, but we all have things that make us feel at peace with ourselves. A focus on taking care of ourselves is a healthy way to feed our inner strength, build self-esteem, and fight stress. Take the time to get to know what renews your energy and nurtures the balance in your life. A clear sense of stability and groundedness will keep you centered when your world gets turned around.

You don't build a bond without being present.

- James Earl Jones

2. Be truly present with others

Whatever obstacles you're facing, you're not alone. The people around you are sources of information and support, just as you are for them. Reach out to the people around you, pay mind to what they say and the actions they take. Everyone handles challenges differently, and you never know what perspectives and approaches others can bring to the table.

Even the most considerate and strongest among us are prone to succumb to the hubbub of busy schedules, other people's drama and individual concerns. When we get pulled into the craziness around us, we tend to lose touch with our own intentions and we may dismiss the diversity of opinions and interactions which enrich our daily lives. We might not always notice, but when we get swept up in our own projects and priorities, other people notice. Don't get me wrong, having focus and direction in your ambitions is necessary, just make sure that when conversing with your friends and coworkers, you're not "checked out" wondering about your to-do list, or how you're going to make your next deadline.

Quality time isn't only a love language, it's also a work language, a leadership language, and a life language, expressing to those around you that you care about them and the role they play for you, be it professional or otherwise.

Being present with others isn't a skill one has to acquire, it's a mindset. There's no better way to show engagement than to be present in the moment. Make time to connect with the people you spend your day with, try not to take their presence for granted. Commit to actively listening to the people you share space with, and remind yourself that they have something to teach you. Your own priorities will still be there later, and your interest and investment in the company of others will be noted and appreciated.

It's the little things that make life BIG!!

3. Take time to enjoy the little things in life

Despite what your interviewer would have you believe, life isn't all about your five-year plan. It isn't even about your two-year plan. Life is made up of little moments of value and intrigue which are overlooked by those who look too far in advance. This is not to say that one shouldn't plan ahead, only that in making those plans, remember to factor in time to appreciate the little things.

When you're organizing your day, take a moment to ask yourself: what does my two-hour plan look like? How about my ten-minute plan? Do I have time in between meetings to simply think or to connect with others? Does it include something that makes me smile? Can I carve out the time to finish that conversation with my coworker about her dogs? Would I feel better after a cup of coffee? By taking the time to indulge in life's little pleasures, you disarm the feckless allure of distraction and procrastination when it's crunch time.

Although at times it may feel like it, life isn't a sprint; it's a hike. While you may be trekking uphill, take the time to appreciate the view, the flora, the wildlife... The little things are lost on those who rush past, and for such people, burnout is inevitable. Stop every now and then - take a deep breath., enjoy the moment. You'll get there eventually.

The little things (or moments) in life are often the most important moments of all!

all we have is now

89% of workers at companies that support well-being initiatives are more likely to recommend their company as a good place to work." — *Forbes (2019)*

free water

4. Be mindful of your health

If you've ever tried to tackle an obstacle on an empty stomach or a poor night's sleep, you know that health plays a huge role in success. Your mind and your body work in tandem, and if one isn't well, you can be sure that the other won't work at its full potential. A healthy diet, consistent exercise, and sufficient REM sleep will make a world of difference to your reactivity and productivity when it's crunch time.

Health consciousness has tangible results in professional performance and can be encouraged by workplaces in an effort to care for and support employees. In 2019, Forbes published statistics stating that "89% of workers at companies that support well-being initiatives are more likely to recommend their company as a good place to work."(1)

How can companies do this? Willis Towers Watson, a leading global advisory firm, found that standalone wellness programs are much less effective in impacting employee well-being than companies which integrate aspects of healthy living into the everyday work environment.(1, 2) This cohesive integration could include more nutritious food options in the cafeteria or break room, improvements to chairs, desks, and lighting, or even on-sight health professionals to support employees' wellness on a daily basis. In any case, making workers feel supported in fostering a healthy lifestyle brings the company focus back to the employee, and demonstrates a genuine concern for workers beyond profit generation.

- our team fosters mental health

Learning without reflection is a waste.
Reflection without. learning is dangerous.

– Confucius

5. Reflect

Stay aware of yourself, your actions, and those around you. Adopting a considered approach to challenges maximizes your ability to respond appropriately and eliminates the unforeseen consequences of thoughtless reaction. Thoughtful responses can only be achieved through reflection and self awareness. If it's true that hindsight is 20/20, just think of how many catastrophes one could avoid by reflecting upon one's past actions and learning from them. Consider making your foresight 20/20! As easy as that might sound, reflection requires time and mindfulness and must be practiced like any other skill in order to be effective. Think about your role in the various spaces you occupy... Do your words and actions match your purpose? How do the people around you respond to your presence in that space? How does this knowledge inform you ? Can better serve them and accomplish your goals in that situation?

Intuition can only get you so far without reflection. If something doesn't feel right, it probably merits consideration before you continue along your path. Taking a moment to reflect upon your feelings, the work you do, or the people you communicate with can help you react accordingly and save you from being blindsided or overwhelmed. It can also be your opportunity to take a deep breath, slow down, and be in the moment when it's tempting to let life get ahead of you.

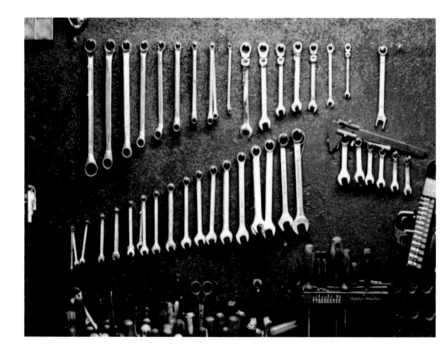

Give us the tools, and we will finish the job.

– Winston Churchill

6. Develop new skills

The world we live in isn't set in stone. Resilience means adapting to changing circumstances, and sometimes new situations require new skill sets. Technology's changing? Have a coworker help you learn a new program. Your team isn't communicating effectively? Brush up on some facilitation and management skills to help them stay on track. It may be tempting to delegate all tasks which challenge us and to take on new colleagues or employees to fill the holes in our own capabilities. While delegation is a commendable and effective leadership tool, before outsourcing new skills, evaluate your reasons for delegating. Are you really doing so to save time and efficiency, or might it be because the prospect of learning those skills intimidates you? How might your management of those team-members and employees be improved if you learned the skills yourself and understood the nature and quality of the work involved?

Learning new skills doesn't mean you have to do everything yourself, but it does maximize your ability to manage and collaborate with others when it comes to dealing with inevitable challenges. Think of your mind as a massive toolbox which you can keep adding to over time. Don't worry if you're not an expert with the electric drill — there are plenty of people around who can lend a hand, but having knowledge and experience with that drill in your toolbox will add to your value and resourcefulness. That knowledge and skill may even one day save you loads of time and fiddling with the wrong tool!

Any obstacle can be overcome; it's just a matter of equipping yourself with the right set of tools.

An unfortunate thing about this world is that the good habits
are much easier to give up than the bad ones.

– W. Somerset Maugham

7. Develop positive habits

Little changes can go a long way when facing bigger challenges. Having positive habits already in place can make even gargantuan tasks much more manageable. Just think how much less intimidating that upcoming presentation would be if you knew in advance that you wouldn't procrastinate, that you'd manage your time effectively, and that you and your colleagues would openly communicate expectations and concerns to each other beforehand!

Want to know the kicker? Positive habits are not difficult to install in your mind, no software or apps to download. Just like any goal, the hardest thing about practicing changing habits and starting positive behaviors is committing to them in the first place. You may find that after a couple weeks of daily effort, you'll start engaging in these behaviors without even thinking about it. This is because without realizing it, you've formed a routine. After a short period of time making a conscious effort to work a certain way, your mind has grown accustomed to those behaviors and considers them the new norm. Things like being proactive, active listening and communication, organization and planning, and self-reflection can all be self-taught. Get into the habit of taking breaks. Check in with yourself about your day. Make to-do lists to stay on track. Routinely show gratitude.

Resilience is much easier when you're not playing catch-up from bad habits.

They say a person needs just three things to be truly happy in this world:

someone to love, something to do, and something to hope for.

— Tom Bodett

8. Find joy every day

There's no stronger candidate for burnout than the person who finds **no joy** in their job or daily life. Indulging in daily joy isn't a luxury reserved for the extrovert, the optimist, and the morning person, and it certainly doesn't imply that you have to be ecstatic all the time. Life continually gifts us little moments of reprieve, even in the most dreary and banal of days. Maybe the traffic jam on your morning commute makes you catch your favorite song on the radio or buys you an extra ten minutes to finish your podcast. Perhaps the latte art in your morning coffee is particularly Instagram-worthy. You might notice that the holiday decorations have gone up at work or that the weather is particularly nice on your lunch break. Don't let the work week get away from you without celebrating unplanned joyful moments.

Whether it be spending time with loved ones or finding the a new podcast or discovering the perfect playlist for your Monday morning office vibes, taking joy in little things is vital to getting through the day. This largely comes down to perception. There's often no circumstantial difference between the lives of the joyful and the morose, but those who find pleasure on a regular basis are making a choice to be happy. Happiness will carry them through the inevitable rough patches of life. Try to have something to look forward to even on the hard days.

Little nuggets of positivity are the best antidote to burnout.

Our potential is one thing. What we do with it is quite another.

- Angela Duckworth

9. Apply yourself

You have skills. Use them. Don't sell yourself short with half-hearted work. This goes for your personal life as well as your career. The more effort you put into a relationship or project, the more you will get out of it in return. Eliminating distractions and staying on task is a great first step in maximizing your efficiency, and will help you achieve the best results for your time. Letting yourself get sidetracked by trivial distractions is the surest way to stress yourself out as you realize how many hours, days, or even weeks you've spent on a task without having made any real progress. Addressing the lack of progress may mean turning off social media while you're at work, establishing periods of "no-contact" with friends, or finding a work environment which is most conducive to your focus.

If you're going to commit time to something, be ready to commit just as much effort. There's no use in getting discouraged by failed attempts; be tenacious in your self-application, and allow yourself to learn from your mistakes. Resilience is not automatic, it takes concerted effort! Don't be afraid to give it your all and see what you're made of. You may very well surprise yourself.

Enthusiasm is common. Endurance is rare.

– Angela Duckworth

10. Work hard

You can diligently practice all 51 of the other recommendations in this book and get nowhere without this one. Resilience only occurs when you have put in effort, encountered obstacles, and worked to overcome them. Therefore, by definition, resilience cannot exist without hard work. Think of it this way: you are a mine of untapped resources. You have knowledge, experience, skills, training, assets, ideas, and passions, but none of these are any good to you or those around you if you don't use them. You are the only one with the capacity to convert your potential into progress, and this can only be done by committing yourself to the task at hand.

This is not to say that you have to be on the job 24/7, hard work is as much about quality as it is quantity, (see tip #9 on Applying Yourself), and you must know that very little will be achieved by those who are not willing to put in the work. To maximize results, couple working hard with working well; focus on time management and prioritization, and when you do find your groove, run with it!

So much quality work can be accomplished in those endorphin-filled productivity kicks! Only you can determine how much work is healthy for you.

All this means is that when it's time to put your nose to the grindstone, you give it your all.

worker smarter
not harder

"Intuition is always right in at least two important ways; it is always in response to something. It always has your best interest at heart."

Gavin De Becker, The Gift of Fear: Survival Signals that Protect Us from Violence

11. Follow your instincts

Intuition is one of your greatest tools in resilience. Only you know when something feels right...and when it doesn't. Nobody else has the power to tell you if you're being treated fairly or if a project aligns with your values. As you reflect, pay attention to your gut and any uneasiness you feel; it may indicate that it's time for a change. On the contrary, if you feel that you've found your calling or that a particular relationship holds the potential for positivity, don't be afraid to nurture those connections.

Author and speaker Gavin De Becker discusses intuition in his book, The Gift of Fear: Survival Signals That Protect Us from Violence.(1) I find his assessment particularly poignant: "Intuition is always right in at least two important ways; it is always in response to something. It always has your best interest at heart."

I like to think of instinct as our own personal advisor that we get to carry around with us everywhere we go. We can ignore the voice urging us to do or not to do something, but chances are, we're better off taking the tip. Sometimes, this voice is silent. These are the times when we get to fall back on careful consideration and critical analysis to make our decisions. However, when our intuition kicks in and we feel drawn to make a certain choice, it's usually an indication that our subconscious has picked up on something that our cognition has missed, and we'd be well-advised to trust it!

learning to listen when anxiety is LOUD.

The Cul-de-Sac (French for "dead end") ... is a situation where you work

and work and work and nothing much changes"

— Seth Godin, The Dip

12. Know when it's time to quit

One of the greatest misconceptions about resilience is that one must never give up. Contrary to popular belief, giving up can be a central step to moving forward and seeking positivity and fulfillment. Resilience means more than sticking with something that your instincts tell you not to pursue -- resilience is about you and your ability to bounce back in life and choose your battles carefully. There's no two ways about it, when you're unhappy in a job, relationship, or project, you are not working at full capacity. It's very difficult to do your best work and be your best self in an environment in which you feel stifled or consistently frustrated.

Everybody experiences negative feelings from time to time, no matter how ideal their situation. Challenges are to be expected, and of course we need t be prepared to face them head on. However the time may come when you reach a point when you realize that your value is not being mobilized effectively and you could accomplish more in a new environment or with a new purpose. Sometimes you find yourself not being valued, you give more than you get, or your well-being is compromised. Just as ducks and geese instinctively know when it's time to fly South for the winter, you must listen to your inner voice and acknowledge when you've given your all and it's time to quit.

Seeking fulfillment where you are a valued resource is its own exercise in resilience.

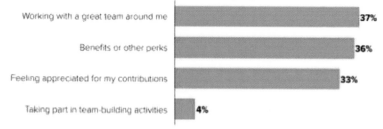

Main Reasons for Staying with an Employer

Working with a great team around me	37%
Benefits or other perks	36%
Feeling appreciated for my contributions	33%
Taking part in team-building activities	4%

Employee's report that one of the most important reason's for staying with their current company is the positive working relationships with those around them.

– Gusto Research Study

13. Seek out kindred spirits

Endurance is much more feasible and even enjoyable when working with people who share your values and who motivate you to continue. Build a support network of individuals or groups who understand and are open to and support your ideas. People who inspire you and support you as you weather the storms you encounter are essential to your resilience. Your support system will help you and will be there for you when the going gets tough. Key people in your life can help you or even challenge you to focus on the purpose of your life's work.

On the other hand, if you don't identify strongly with your organization's mission or culture, or get along with your team, your defenses against frustration, pressure, and apathy are reduced, and burnout is almost inevitable. A study by Gusto (the results of which are shown on the previous page), found that almost 40% of survey respondents felt that the most important reason for staying with their current company was their positive working relationship with those around them.(1)

> For millions of years, human beings have been part of one tribe or another. A group needs only two things to be a tribe: a shared interest and a way to communicate.
>
> *Seth Godin, Tribes; We need you to lead us.*

In wisdom gathered over time I have found

that every experience is a form of exploration.

– Ansel Adams

14. Explore new places

It's true what they say, sometimes a change is as good as a rest. Familiarizing yourself with a new environment can make a major difference in the way you perceive everyday life and work. It's very easy to imagine the world as an extension of your office or comfort zone, but a step outside into another building, country, community, or field of work can provide perspective and refresh your mind.

One of my personal favorite things about my job as a corporate trainer and leadership development facilitator is that I get the opportunity to travel around the world and work in diverse environments. The ability to explore new places and communities gives me a blank slate for creativity and personal development every time I set foot outside of my beloved San Diego bubble. I also cannot express the degree to which travel and change inform my lessons and values, and as a result are reflected in my work.

You don't need to be a world traveler to take advantage of exploring new places as an avenue to resilience. For remote workers, this could be as easy as getting out of the house and working from a new wifi cafe. For office-goers, consider capitalizing on any work trip opportunities, and practice using your time off (weekends, evenings, holidays) to venture into new areas of town, attend cultural events or take day-trips when possible. Shake up your commute to work every now and then to break up the monotony of your daily routine and introduce intrigue to your schedule. The brain is a muscle which can get idle and lax if not stimulated with occasional novelty, and a change of scene can be a great antidote to a flabby brain.

We meet aliens every day who have something to give us.

They come in the form of people with different opinions.

– William Shatner

15. Be open to different opinions

This tip is a resilience fundamental. Being too set in your ways and invested in a single viewpoint or path makes it difficult to adapt to shifting circumstances. Different people have unique experiences which inform their opinions. Your experience may be correct for you, but in order to lead and collaborate with diverse groups, it's vital to be open to equally diverse ideas. Understanding the providence of people's differing opinions increases your flexibility and makes you easier to work with.

You may have heard the saying, "boughs that don't bend, break". The same goes for people. The more rigid you are in your views and the less flexible you are with the opinions of others, the more likely you are to snap when things don;t go your way. This "snapping" looks different for everyone, but is likely to come in the form of being irritable and difficult to work with, to burnout and extreme overwhelm. In any case, closing yourself down to diverse viewpoints inhibits your ability to be flexible and bounce back when under pressure.

The best leaders don't lead alone, they are informed by a variety of invested parties whose differing perspectives offer balance and nuance to their actions. This is not to say that you have to agree with all the opinions you encounter, (this would be impossible and would imply that you have no real opinions of your own), but rather that an appreciation for the inherent value in diversity better equips you to handle adversity and navigate dissonance in your team.

The extent of your consciousness is limited only by your ability to love

and to embrace with your love the space around you, and all it contains.

– Napoleon Bonaparte

16. Embrace your loved ones

As much as we might like to think we are independent and self sufficient, we are not work machines. Love and tenderness in its many forms keeps us human and fuels our ability to make it to the end of every day. Don't be afraid to keep your loved ones close and display your affection for them on a regular basis. These relationships are the ones we need to fall back on when things don't go our way.

As a mother of three beautiful children, family is central to my life and identity. Being there for my loved ones and counting on them to be there for me has provided me with perspective and balance in my career and reinforced my belief in the power of community and human resilience. Interestingly, although one of the first things we ask upon meeting someone is what they do for a living, it bears mentioning that identity transcends profession. Your sense of self is not limited to your day job, and there's great value in identifying as a mother, sister, brother, friend, uncle, partner -- you name it. Placing emphasis and importance on your loved ones and the roles you play in each other's lives does not detract from your professionalism, and there's no shame in putting family and friends first... quite the opposite, be proud of great relationships in your life.

Gratitude is not a limited resource, nor is it costly. It is abundant as air.

We breathe it in but forget to exhale.

— Marshall Goldsmith

17. Thank the people who support you

Resilience isn't a one-person show. People in your life will help and support you along the way, and this does not in any way detract from your accomplishments. However, it is important to take a moment to thank those who have had your back, as you may need to lean on their support and resources in the future. (Not only this, but everyone deserves recognition for their efforts, and if you can be a decent and grateful human being, why not, right?)

I'm a strong believer that robust leadership is less about authority than it is about connection and communication. Consistently thanking your team for their support and recognizing their efforts builds mutual trust and reinforces your colleagues' faith in your leadership. People are generally willing to go to incredible lengths in service of those who show appreciation. On the other hand, there's no surer way to disincentivize hard work than letting people feel that their efforts go unacknowledged.

Think back on the number of times you gave someone your all, whether in your personal or professional life, and weren't properly thanked for your time and trouble. Now take a moment to reflect back on a time in which you felt truly appreciated for your endeavors, and were explicitly thanked for your support. In which instance did you feel most strongly motivated to go the extra mile again? Chances are, you were much happier to put in the hours in the second instance than in the first. Remember, people are predictable -- we like to be recognized when we lend our support to others. You alone make the difference between the first scenario and the second for those around you, and the likelihood of them continuing to pull for your success lies largely in your hands.

Anybody who succeeds is helping people. The secret to success is find a need and fill it; find a hurt and heal it; find a problem and solve it.

– Robert H. Schuller

18. Be there for others

Everyone can use a helping hand every now and again, and by being there for those around you, you deepen your ties to the community and build rapport with the people in your life. This doesn't only go for people with whom you see eye to eye; sometimes being there for people you disagree with reaps the greatest rewards, as it shows compassion and leadership, and may pave the way for more flexibility and positive collaboration in the future.

For me, this one has largely manifested itself in my balance between motherhood and professionalism. As a mother of three wonderful children, there are times when I am called upon to be there for my kids and put family first. I believe that this doesn't make me any less of a businesswoman; if anything, it makes me a better one. The ability to balance the priorities of family and work is a point of pride in my career, this precarious balance hinges upon values of compassion, equilibrium, and leadership. Furthermore, I've come to notice that the times when I get to be there for those I care about, others also step in to be there and support me. I can't count the number of times my team members have stepped up to cover a class for me, or my colleagues have worked extra hours so I could take care of what I needed to do. That's the beauty of community -- when you're there for others, they will be there for you.

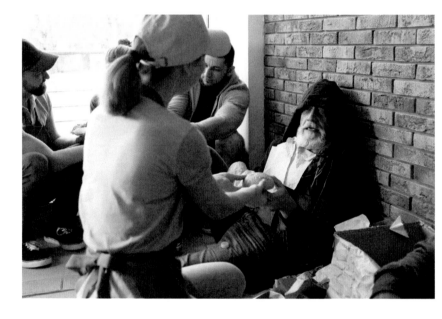

We make a living by what we get, and we make a life by what we give.

- Winston Churchill

19. Give back

Exhibit generosity. Leverage synergy. People will be much more inclined to go the extra mile for you if they feel that you would do the same for them. Give favors, accept favors -- and make sure that when the time comes for you to lend a hand to others, do your best work, don't cut corners. Mutually-beneficial relationships are always the most robust and fulfilling, and by giving back you not only do the right thing, you also maximize your potential.

Giving back is especially important for those of us in positions of leadership and management. It's necessary and healthy to regularly take a step back and acknowledge how much our teams do for us on a daily basis. These moments provide excellent opportunities to think of ways to give back to those who support us in our lives and work. Staff appreciation days, after-hours office events, and tokens of appreciation for a job well-done can all be great ways of showing appreciation to those who throw weight behind our vision.

In terms of giving back, think outside the box. Think about the charities and organizations that reflect your values and advocate for the things that are important to you. Don't overlook these groups when the opportunity arises to give back. Donate your time, resources, or funds to good causes, this goes a long way as a show of solidarity and communicates a positive message in your community.

With mindfulness, you can establish yourself in the present in order
to touch the wonders of life that are available in that moment.

– Thich Nhat Hanh

20. Practice mindfulness

Leading meditation publication, *Mindful*, defines mindfulness as "the basic human ability to be fully present, aware of where we are and what we're doing, and not overly reactive or overwhelmed by what's going on around us."(1)

The ability to be present and manage our reactivity is central to the practice of resilience, as it keeps us grounded in our reality and allows us better to navigate obstacles as they arise. Mindfulness is closely tied to intention and purpose, and can be achieved either through formal meditation, or by being increasingly aware of one's actions, emotions, and senses.

Think of mindfulness as the art of paying more attention to everything you do, from your morning routine to your most strenuous events of the day. By being mindful of the little things you do on a daily basis, you can reclaim all the actions and motions you otherwise take for granted, and in doing so, you will reassert your sense of self.

In addition to your inner-self, mindfulness can be incorporated into the way we interact with the world around us. It's very easy to get wrapped up in our own work and priorities, and yet getting caught up in the busyness of life can impede our ability to respond effectively to change. Staying mindful of those around us and the space we occupy in a team or community makes us better team players and more adaptable as groups.

Remember that you are not an island and that your work is part of a greater effort in which everyone plays a role. Pay attention to the people you interact with, and be mindful of how you can help each other accomplish your goals.

"Take a big, slow inhale. Hold it for three seconds, then, placing your top front teeth on your bottom lip, release a passive exhale. Your exhale should take at least twice as long as your inhale. At the bottom of the exhale, pause for a moment, then repeat."

Business Insider

21. Breathe

Among the strongest antidotes to getting overwhelmed is the art of steady breathing. Take time out of your day to sit back and inhale some deep breaths. Deep breathing increases the flow of oxygen to the brain and diffuses the buildup of stress. Although some of us may think of meditative breathing as a holistic pseudoscience on par with numerology or reflexology, improper breathing has very real consequences for our health and daily performance; the consequences include such things as migraines, back aches, and chronic fatigue.(1)

Breathing exercises are a great wellness trick to work into your schedule, and will help you think clearly in the midst of anxiety and pressure. Back in 2013, Business Insider published an article featuring a number of breathing exercises for maximizing wellness and performance, and they have become central to my daily routine ever since.(1) One in particular stuck with me as a quick fix for stress and burnout:

Just like many breathing exercises, the technique above lowers the heart rate and re-centers you, making it an ideal life hack under pressure! Integrating tricks like this into my everyday life have made me more conscious of my breath and has reduced the tension I carry. Take a step back, take a deep breath, and lighten your load for the day!

If you put yourself in a position where you have to stretch outside your comfort zone, then you are forced to expand your consciousness.

– Les Brown

22. Stretch Yourself

Literally, stretch!! Physical alignment is closely tied to mental strength and resilience. The intricate network of nerves and synapses which connect our bodies and brains mean that if there's a dis-accord or sense of discomfort in the body, it's likely to effect the way the mind functions. Misalignment often manifests itself as restlessness, distraction, irritation, or lack of focus, all of which can be alleviated at least somewhat by paying closer attention to what our bodies are telling us. During those moments of awareness, changing position or stretching is a great way to keep the body engaged after a long period of sitting still.

Health experts say that sitting is the new smoking! So, stand up and take a walk around the room, the office or the block - stretch out your arms and legs as you go. The increased blood flow and movement will help release the tension that has built up in your body and improve your posture along the way. I find it's very easy in a busy workday to forget to stretch, and to lose track of time completely, especially when I've been sitting at my desk, glued to my computer, so I've always been a strong proponent of standing desks for able-bodied folks, back supports, and exercise balls to keep the body aligned and engaged during work hours.

> Research shows that you can reduce your chances of cancer, type 2 diabetes, cardiovascular disease, and back pain, all with one simple lifestyle change: reduce the time you spend sitting..
>
> *https://www.startstanding.org/sitting-new-smoking/#*

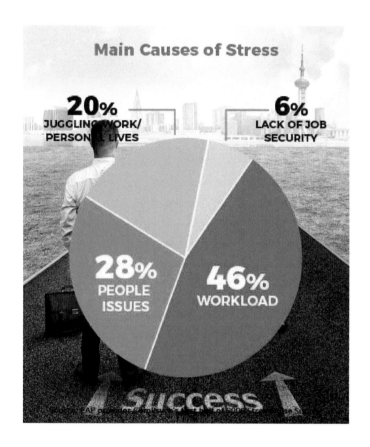

23. Relax

There are moments when it's go time and there are also moments when it's not. The moments between tasks or projects, after successful meetings, on lunch break. In these moments, it's important to take advantage of the tranquility, and to switch off for a while. Without relaxation, work and stress build up and overwhelm us, stifling our efficiency. People are like computers in this regard -- sometimes we get backed up and run slower than usual because of the quantity or intensity of work we're trying to process. When this happens, the best thing you can do for your computer is to switch it off, let it cool down, and power it up again later. The same goes for you. When we reach capacity for our workload or attention span, tasks which would otherwise be manageable appear insurmountable, and rebooting with a little relaxation and recovery makes a big difference in our efficiency and overall well-being.

The American Institute of Stress reports that that workload accounts for 46% of the stress the average person carries on a daily basis, meaning that if we learn to better manage our workloads and professional pressures, we can reduce our overall stress levels by almost half.(1) Be sure to capitalize on your weekends, days off, and little moments of reprieve throughout the day to recharge and reset. You will work better when you power back on again.

I was taken by the power that savoring a simple cup of

coffee can have to connect people and create community.

– Howard Schultz

24. Connect

Connect with people. Connect ideas. Connect with different departments at your office. People and ideas don't exist in a vacuum; everything is interrelated, and practicing connectivity keeps us in touch with the dynamic world around us. Understanding the connections between people and ideas is a key factor in building resourcefulness and adaptability.

One of the most efficient ways of achieving connection is through networking. Fostering relationships and connections with the people we meet, no matter how cursory, exponentially expands the wealth of knowledge and resources to which we have access and broadens the possibilities of what we can accomplish. I owe a lot of my success and progress to formal networking -- that is good old-fashioned, face-to-face people-collecting! If you keep an eye out, you'll find that networking events are everywhere, and have a ton to offer by way of professional and community connections. Alternatively, always carrying business cards featuring your name and contact information and your favorite skill set - give them to people you vibe with, new acquaintances, or anyone whose experience interests you.... then follow up!

Not an extrovert? Not a problem! One of the benefits of this incredible age of technology we live in is that a lot of inter-connectivity and networking can be achieved without ever leaving your desk. LinkedIn is a fantastic resource for this, as are the bountiful social media platforms we enjoy. Don't be afraid to reach out to friends and acquaintances to leverage their connections as well -- the wider your circle, the higher your chances of finding the right person to lend a hand when the time comes. In general, I've found that people like to be of service and are more than happy to offer their support to those who ask kindly. Use these connections to make sense of your work, and build a team of people and resources to support you. You will improve your resilience significantly if you understand how people and things connect to one another, and can influence the outcome of your work.

If you take responsibility for yourself you will develop a hunger to accomplish your dreams.

– Les Brown

25. Develop yourself

No matter what tasks come across your desk, YOU are always your greatest project. You are a fluid, dynamic force of skill and personality which can be improved upon and developed every day. Budget and finance may curtail your resources in work initiatives, but the sky's the limit in how much you invest in developing yourself. Learning a new skill or rethinking a bad habit are great ways of improving yourself as a person and colleague.

> ## All of the secrets to life are kept between the covers of books.
>
> *- Vey Linville*

There's nothing wrong with having areas of development, and having a sound grasp on your strengths and weaknesses is healthy, as any interviewer will tell you! Nobody is perfectly rounded in their skills and qualities, meaning that everyone has areas to improve upon. This isn't something to be insecure about; think of it instead as a perpetual opportunity to build the best version of yourself you can be.

Work on taking constructive criticism as pointers on where to concentrate your self-development without getting caught up in the whirlwind of self-doubt and insecurity. Criticism is only a suggestion, and is only as true as you make it. This said, I find that an extra set of eyes can be refreshing, and before I allow myself to get defensive in the face of constructive criticism, I try taking my ego out of the equation. It's not always easy, but once I open myself up to the idea of development and remember that I'm still learning, I become much more flexible and able to improve myself as a person, boss, leader, mother or any other role I have. If you're not sure where to start, go back and reread tip #5 on reflection, and see what areas of development emerge.

You must be the change you wish to see in the world.

– Mahatma Gandhi

26. Be willing to change

If improving yourself means change, then embrace it. Nobody is forcing you to be someone other than yourself; you're just expanding the possibilities of what being yourself can mean. The world today is in a state of constant change, with trends of globalization, technology, communication, politics, and culture, altering our reality sometimes faster than we realize. The speed of change makes it difficult for the average person to keep up with circumstances and environments which are continuously in flux. The people who thrive will be those who can adapt and thrive demonstrating resilience in the face of the unexpected.

In order to do thrive, it's vital to be open to change not only in the world around you, but also in yourself. In many ways these changes can be freeing. We're not bound to the people we have been in the past, or to any of the habits or worldviews which once held us back. Instead, we are at liberty to embrace new ideas in response to new information, and evolve our actions, beliefs, and behaviors to accommodate increasingly diversified and dynamic surroundings.

Sometimes, we don't even have to look on a global scale to find incentive to change; there are times when in order to be there for someone we care for or to fulfill a particular role for somebody, we have to change things about ourselves to be the person others need us to be. As long as you're not compromising any of your core values or being untrue to yourself, there's nothing wrong with stepping out of your comfort zone and revisiting the way you behave in a given situation (perhaps talking less and listening more, taking the lead more readily, taking a backseat to a project, choosing your battles, practicing new forms of tolerance, etc). Don't be afraid to embrace the world's tendency to change... you will prove much more resilient in the long run if you allow yourself to change with it.

Live and allow others to live; hurt no one; life is dear to all living beings.

- Mahavira

27. Allow others to be who they are

Everyone has something unique to bring to a community. You have immense value in the space you occupy, with your own perspectives and experiences -- but so does everybody else. Don't be too hasty to judge or discount the identities of those around you, or you risk alienating the very people you may later rely on to overcome your obstacles.

Imagine a football field. Each team has eleven players on the field at any given moment, and everyone has a distinct perspective, identity, and skill set to bring to their assigned role. An offense made entirely of players built like wide receivers (typically slim, lean, and light-footed) wouldn't last ten minutes against a decent defense line-up. By the same token, a team comprising entirely of linebackers (typically muscle-dense, stocky, and strong) would never be able to keep pace with its opponents. You don't have to know anything about football to recognize the synergy that results from team diversity. No two players on the field have the exact same priorities or strengths, but the team performs at its best when everyone is allowed to be exactly who they are and bring their unique abilities to the game.

Whether in athletics, work, or social life, diversity is among the greatest assets of any team. Don't sell yourself short by rejecting people who are different from you and who even challenge your thinking - these individuals are all valuable in our life.

One who gains strength by overcoming obstacles possesses the only strength
which can overcome adversity.

– Albert Schweitzer

28. Look past the obstacles

It goes without saying that the challenges everyone faces are valid and pressing, but as they say, " *This, too, shall pass.*" Try not to get too caught up in your current obstacles and lose sight of the bigger picture. You're doing what you do for a reason. All of your amalgamated efforts up to this point have led you to this very moment. You have probably fought tooth and nail for the opportunity to make the most of today, and energy spent stressing about the little things is energy that could be better invested in preparing for longer-term goals.

It's also worth mentioning here that many of the obstacles we struggle with on a regular basis can be easily resolved through diligent organization. Time management, when well-executed, can make a world of difference in meeting deadlines and structuring stress-free work days. Similarly, breaking down daunting projects into smaller, more manageable tasks helps us stay on schedule and chip away at larger goals. It's much easier to see our own progress when we're not bogged down in the weeds of small challenges. Keeping an eye on the bigger picture will help you stay focused on your purpose and motivation and may even give you insight into how to handle your current obstacles.

You may be struggling to win your current challenge, but don't lose sight of the greater end goal you are working to achieve!

Businesses that encourage and prioritize employee collaboration are found to be five times more likely to have significantly higher rates of performance over their less collaborative counterparts.

Institute for Corporate Productivity

29. Collaborate for synergy

Synergy occurs when people or ideas come together to create a whole that is greater than the sum of its parts, think 1+1=85! Just as everyone has something different to contribute to a situation, those contributions can be pooled together to create a greater result than they ever could have achieved individually. The only way to achieve this maximum potential of skills and resources is through collaboration.

Collaboration and teamwork are more than buzzwords companies throw around to flaunt their community values. Statistics highlight the very real and quantifiable benefits of effective synergy on productivity and success. A study conducted by Salesforce on employee collaboration reported that 85% of respondents believe that lack of collaboration and poor communication are the primary reason for failed projects and overall workplace failures.(1) Conversely, according to the Institute for Corporate Productivity, businesses that encourage and prioritize employee collaboration are found to be five times more likely to have significantly higher rates of performance over their less collaborative counterparts.(1) The very presence of a collaborative corporate culture, makes a world of difference to the quality of our work as well as our motivation and morale to stay on task.

You may be a powerhouse alone, but just think how much more powerful your assets and strengths could be when joined with others!

"American culture in particular has instilled in us the bizarre notion that to ask for help amounts to an admission of failure. But some of the most powerful, successful, admired people in the world seem, to me, to have something in common: they ask constantly, creatively, compassionately, and gracefully."

Amanda Palmer in The Art of Asking

30. Leverage your resources

Resilience is contingent upon resourcefulness. You may have people, funds, connections, or assets at your disposal which could contribute to your mission, but success lies in whether one leverages those resources effectively.

The first and most vital step to taking advantage of resources is learning to recognize them around us. We are surrounded by potential in everything we do, from the acquaintances we make to the time and money we have to spend, and it's up to us to recognize the value in our environments. Regardless of where you are in your career, you have access to an abundance of resources you can tap into. If you're well established and have been in your current position for a long time, fantastic! You likely have teams and colleagues who know you, company support, and a wealth of experience to leverage in order to accomplish your goals. If you're new to the job, brilliant! You have the advantage of external experience, a broader and fresher perspective, and a more diverse network of connections to pull from when problem-solving.

Amanda Palmer, world-renowned rockstar-turned-author, and one of my personal favorite figureheads of resilience, discusses the subject of social resourcefulness in her memoir, *The Art of Asking* (1), she beautifully demonstrates that asking for help is a sign of strength, not weakness – I have heard this repeated from front line leaders to Fortune 50 executives.

We build too many walls and not enough bridges.

– Isaac Newton

31. Build bridges - not walls

Connectivity goes a long way in life, with the unique power to break down obstacles that appear insurmountable to us as individuals. By joining forces with others and forming connections across geographic, ideological, and cultural barriers, we maximize our power to effect change and overcome communal challenges. Many aspects of our current political climate seem hell-bent on dividing us rather than bringing us together and cultivating our strengths and similarities. As a result, many people limit their horizons by isolating themselves from groups and ideas with which they are unfamiliar or uncomfortable.

Collectively, we can overcome this by seeking common ground and connection with diverse people and concepts instead of buying into the narrative of rejection and isolation. Opening lines of communication or "bridges" between groups expands the people and resources we have in the little corner of our world and builds our collective potential to tackle challenges. Closing down and building "walls" can only harm all parties involved by pushing away potential allies and settling for a less informed and developed worldview. By advocating for values of inclusivity and accessibility in our workplaces and social environments, we take small steps in building these bridges.

Make an effort to be a voice of tolerance and community in your space; resilience cannot exist without diversity.

To add value to others, one must first value others.

– John C. Maxwell

32. Add value

Before you can tackle adding value, it's important that you know what value you add. Take time for self reflection and get clear on your strengths and how to present them. Know the going rate for your work in the current economy. Consider what unique qualities you bring to the workspace or relationship, and what holes those qualities fill in your environment. Once you've come to terms with your value and how you fit into the network of people around you, you can begin working on mobilizing that value in everything you do.

In both your interpersonal life and work endeavors, leverage those skills and characteristics that set you apart and take on the roles that only you can do. Think of it this way... you have cornered the market on YOU. Nobody can compete with you at being yourself, and the team or relationship will benefit immensely if you take the initiative to bring your own flare and voice to the table. The diversity and skills that accompany your specific education, work and life experiences, interpersonal skills, knowledge and passions, and physical assets will be an attribute to the environments that you work and play in.

Think about how you can integrate the myriad of strengths into your projects and interactions. In doing so, you will make yourself indispensable!

It's during our darkest moments that we must focus to see the light.

-Aristotle

33. Embrace the micro moments of balance

The stars don't have to align for you to have some balance in life. Even the little moments can make a difference to your day. Take for example the feeling of having answered all your emails and no longer feeling behind, or when someone's helped you with something and you finally get to return the favor, or even something as simple as enjoying a cup of coffee with a colleague on your lunch break. These little moments of peace and balance will ease your way through even the most hectic of weeks, and reduce those pesky stress levels we discussed earlier.

Our brains are wired to appreciate balance and harmony, so when situations arise in which we have closure or at peace, we experience a sense of satisfaction which naturally combats burnout. I have found that these feelings are strongest in moments when I feel like I'm on the same page with someone I work or interact with. That sense of mutual understanding and symbiosis is refreshing, and I often have to take a moment to recognize and celebrate my tiny victory. Give yourself credit where credit is due; don't let the opportunity get away from you, in this moment, you are centered and grounded. You made it happen. There's nothing wrong with stepping back to admire your handiwork and recharge before you tackle the rest of your day.

We can't solve problems by using the same kind of thinking

we used when we created them.

- Albert Einstein

34. Reframe negative situations

Being pessimistic about your situation is the surest way to produce a negative outcome. The results of any situation are largely a product of our perspective going into it. Sometimes, as we all know, things don't go our way but this can often produce new opportunities and occasions for learning. I think it's safe to say that we've all been in interviews in which we've been asked to expand upon times we've handled failure. This is because it's in these moments that our true resilience and inner value jumps out -- or doesn't. When our plans fall through, we get to choose how we respond: whether we accept defeat and self-pity, or whether we look for the positive aspects and turn the situation to our advantage.

Thomas Edison is famous for having said, on the subject of inventing the light-bulb, "*I have not failed. I've just found 10,000 ways that won't work.*" As we are all now aware from our current dependence upon artificial light, Edison did, in fact, succeed in creating the light-bulb. However, if he had gotten discouraged by any of his 10,000 previous attempts, history would have forgotten him entirely, and we may all still be living by candlelight. Edison's perspective, while amusing in its extremity, demonstrates a very achievable mindset which can be cultivated through perseverance and simple positivity. By refusing to view his work process as failure, Edison wasn't being unrealistically optimistic, rather, he was increasing his chances of eventual success by reframing his failures as learning opportunities.

Look for the silver lining (or learning moment) in every challenge; keeping a positive mindset is one of the surest ways to build your resilience.

So many things begin to change when you come at the world

from that perspective of more than one right answer.

– Dewitt Jones , National Geographic Photographer

35. Pay attention to perspective

The beauty of relativity is that the same situation will be viewed differently by different people without losing its integrity. Understanding that an obstacle can be assessed from numerous standpoints allows for a more comprehensive and thorough grasp of the situation and its effect on different groups of people. Considering various perspectives also helps you come to terms with people's differing opinions and how to coordinate with them.

Many factors play into the construction of our individual perspectives, from our culture and upbringing, to our personal experiences and whether we've had lunch on a given day. Our mood, health, knowledge, experience, and history all impact how we view and approach a situation, so don't be surprised if the people around you don't see things exactly the way you do. Instead of viewing this disaccord as an obstacle to collaboration, try interpreting it instead as an asset. Rather than having one cohesive two-dimensional understanding of a situation, a team with numerous perspectives has a deeper, multi-dimensional vision of things with a much more holistic grasp on possible approaches or solutions.

Taking note of the various perspectives in our environment enhances our adaptability to circumstances and strengthens our rapport with team members and loved ones. National Geographic Photographer, Dewitt Jones, speaks about the importance of perspective, and highlights the fact that sometimes you don't capture the best photograph until you look a different direction. Noticing and understanding perspective is a vital step in building open-mindedness and by proxy, making us better communicators and collaborators. As you work on becoming more mindful and practice reflecting as we discussed earlier, think about incorporating perspective into your reflection.

Think about how your own perspective informs your actions, and how you can be more open and accepting with the perspectives of others.

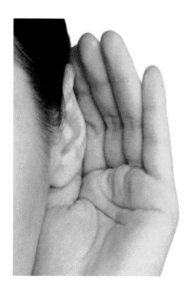 

O Divine Master, grant that I may not so much seek

to be consoled as to console

To be understood, as to understand

To be loved, as to love.

- Prayer of St. Francis

36. Listen first

I know you have something to say, and you deserve the chance to say it. However, before voicing your opinion, try taking a step back and listening to those around you. If you're entering an ongoing conversation or meeting for the first time, make sure to take note of the narratives and voices already being circulated by its participants. Consider the speakers, listen to their respective experiences and viewpoints, and be conscientious of how your input fits into the conversation. Particularly when in discussions about marginalization, personal or systematic struggles, or other such sensitive topics, take a moment to reflect on your place in the conversation. If you are a guest in the space, consider whether your opinion adds value to the conversation and how to interact with the conversation in a meaningful way that respects the narratives of others.

Not only is this a considerate thing to do which makes you a more respectful and effective team player, but it also gives you the advantage of hearing where other people are coming from and phrasing your argument accordingly. Listening first allows you to assess your place in the context of the conversation, strategize, hear any potential opposition, and if you decide to proceed, choose how you want to pitch your point for maximum influence.

Don't judge others,
Work on yourself.

37. Don't judge others immediately

It is said that you never get a second chance t make a good first impression, and there is no doubt that we all make snap judgements about people every day. There are psychological studies quoting "time to judgement" from anywhere between 1/10 of a second to a minute. It's human nature to assess our situation and surroundings, we are wired with an imeddded threat response for self preservation. It's okay to disagree; we all have people that we align with more than others. It is, however, important to refrain from judging those around us to the best of our ability. Judgment breeds hostility in our immediate environment and this tension and lack of mutual understanding will limit those you can turn to in times of need.

It can be challenging to put our judgment in check, think back on our previous discussion of diversity and the value of individuality. When we open ourselves up to a more diverse range of people and ideas, we minimize the negative energy we send out into the world and maximize our potential to accomplish goals and achieve synergy. Again, this doesn't require us to agree with everyone, or to support every aspect of others' lives, but removing our ego from the equation and minding our own business contributes to our own personal growth and increases the value we bring to any team. Employers love people who work well with others for a reason, and this aspect of our character is severely inhibited when we allow ourselves to be consumed by judgment.

Open-mindedness costs nothing, and will significantly increase the returns on your efforts.

Nature's beauty is a gift that cultivates appreciation and gratitude.

- Louie Schwartzberg

38. Savor the beauty of your surroundings

Fight burnout by appreciating the beauty around you. This doesn't only apply to those who live and work in picturesque places (though there's nothing like a view to relieve stress!); everyone can savor the beauty in people, organization, art, cityscapes, you name it. Keeping your senses engaged with beauty is stimulating to your mind and soul and provides little moments of rest and relaxation to get you through the day.

There's a reason we are soothed by social media like Instagram, Facebook, and Tumblr -- we crave the aesthetic to break up the banal. There's no shame in venturing online to appreciate beauty, but try opening yourself up to the little moments of perfection in your everyday life. When we start taking our environment for granted, it affects our mood and capacity for positivity. This in turn impacts our resilience. If we never take the time to appreciate the beauty that surrounds us, we stop noticing our environment all together, and can very easily get bogged down in our own concerns and struggles. By acknowledging aesthetics and appreciating nature, light, architecture, you name it, we are humbled to know that the world retains its beauty and grace, no matter what we are going through.

I travel extensively (which can be quite tiresome), and one of the things I like to do is to take time to appreciate the art I see in the airports I traverse. I post pictures and videos on my Instagram feed of paintings, sculpture, music and other creative displays. This purposeful approach to seek out the beauty I find in unexpected places provides a refreshing mental reset to an otherwise stressful day. Next time you're having a rough day or busy week, take a moment on your lunch break or weekend to count the beautiful things you see. Chances are, you'll end up realizing that almost everything you encounter can be considered beautiful if viewed from the right perspective. Make an effort to keep noticing the aesthetic value around you then pay attention to the impact this can have on your mood going forward.

There is no better than adversity. Every defeat, every heartbreak, every loss, contains its own seed, its own lesson on how to improve your performance the next time.

- Malcolm X

39. Welcome adversity

Good leadership seldom means unchallenged leadership. Nobody can grow and expand their potential as a colleague or community member if they are never challenged or opposed in their ways of thinking. Adversity comes in many forms, be it colleagues who question our authority and competence, or, in my case, the recession of 2008! As a brand new entrepreneur with big dreams, big loans, and a big family to support, adversity couldn't have hit my plans at a tougher time, and I know I wouldn't be the leader I am today if I hadn't had to overcome that hurdle. Conflict and struggle call into question our passion and tenacity. The ability to effectively manage adversity and act with grace and humility when confronted with hardship or conflict winnows out the fair weather leaders from the truly resilient. The learning is in the struggle!

The concept of reframing negative situations with positivity becomes relevant to success. When challenged, try to remember that those who bring adversity into a team are not necessarily enemies to your vision, and are likely bringing up questions you will have to deal with at a later date anyway. These people and situations, while trying, provide us with learning opportunities and test our competence in leadership. Try not to get overwhelmed by these situations, instead embrace the struggle -- you are in your current position for a reason, and exercises in contradiction will equip you to overcome greater obstacles down the road. Addressing adversity head on and embracing its challenges will strengthen your communication and leadership skills and make you a more formidable asset to your team in the future.

He (or she) who is not every day conquering some fear

has not learned the secret of life.

- Ralph Waldo Emerson

40. Conquer your fears

I always try to think of my fears less as weaknesses and more as superpowers I haven't unlocked yet. Focusing on our potential for improvement instead of our current inhibitions changes the voice in our head from discouraging to encouraging. Afraid of confrontation? Just think how much more you'll be able to accomplish when you overcome this fear and become more comfortable with self-advocacy! Nervous about failing? Imagine how freeing it will feel when you can finally tackle projects with the confidence that it's okay not to succeed the first time around. Or the second. Or the tenth.

I am a staunch believer that the most difficult part of any project or obstacle is committing to the initial will to overcome it. The first step is always the hardest, and giving in to deeply-rooted insecurities and fears of failure inhibit us from taking that initial step toward progress. You've probably heard the Wayne Gretzky quote, "*You miss 100% of the shots you don't take.*" It's natural to have fears; even the most courageous and successful individuals have them. Gretzky's quote speaks specifically to those who let those fears stand in the way of their actions. Instead of letting your phobias and concerns dictate your actions, try letting them inform your actions. There's nothing wrong with taking extra precautions, or using your fears as motivation to prepare and strategize.

Make sure that when the opportunity presents itself for you to act, you take the shot.

The only thing worse than being blind is having sight but no vision.

- Helen Keller

41. Clarify your vision

Seize the time and space to reflect on what you want out of your career, workplace or relationship. Ask yourself where you see this process going and what you hope to learn from it along the way. It's important to check in with yourself regularly to make sure you're staying true to your ambitions and values and on track for your desired path. Clarifying your vision and expectations will help you stay on track on a day-to-day basis and will keep the bigger picture in focus. It's okay to re-focus your vision; it's healthy to update your goals. None of us are exactly the same people we were a few years ago, our wants and needs all the same as in years past -- such is the way of personal growth and development. It's normal for our vision and aspirations to change accordingly.

It may help to keep a vision journal, which you can revisit and add to with things that inspire you, schedule goals and deadlines, and jot down any thoughts about your experience in work and your life path. Externalizing our thoughts in journals or conversations with close friends helps us to better process our emotions and ideas, and keeping track of dreams and inspirations in a journal we can return to and review is a fun and efficient way of ensuring we're on the right track for our personal aspirations.

It's okay if your focus changes, just make sure to stay true to your values and beliefs - keep checking in with yourself and live your intentions.

The spider's web: She finds an innocuous corner in which to spin her web.

The longer the web takes, the more fabulous its construction.

- Donna Lynn Hope

42. Tackle big goals

There's no need to live in fear of your ambitions. Don't fall into the trap of tackling little tasks upfront and procrastinating on the big goals. Procrastination is the surest way to ensure your goals never get achieved. Instead, break down your big goals into smaller steps and determine what manageable tasks you can accomplish every day to advance your progress on your big goals.

Every major project is made up of a series of interim steps which contribute to the greater goal. For a long time, the idea of writing a book was incredibly daunting to me. I knew it was something I wanted to do; I had so much to say, so many lessons and experiences to share with the world, but I put off the goal of writing my first book because I'd gotten into a funk of thinking of it as a finished product, and the finished product intimidated me. It wasn't until I broke down that vision into manageable tasks that I could check off in my planner that my goal began finally began coming together. Over time, I stopped thinking of it as a book and started to think of it as an outline. A page. A chapter. And lo and behold, a book started taking form.

Whether your big goals are writing a book, starting a business, getting a degree, getting into shape, or spending more time with family, they won't happen on their own. Take the first steps and get the ball rolling. Make a schedule with milestones so you can track your progress. Above all, be patient with yourself. As Jodi Picoult so eloquently put it... "
You might not write well every day, but you can always edit a bad page. You can't edit a blank page."

The only way to keep your health is to eat what you don't want,

drink what you don't like, and do what you'd rather not.

- Mark Twain

43. Get healthy

Eat healthy. Drink water. Meditate. Make time to exercise. Get more sleep. Improve your posture with a standing desk or back support. This doesn't have to be a gargantuan undertaking or investment; physical health can be improved by any number of small alterations to our lifestyles which make a world of difference to our efficiency at work and general wellness. The journal Population Health Management finds that tobacco use, lack of exercise, and poor eating habits were major indicators of poor employee productivity.(1) Health and wellness have also always been key ingredients to my recipe for resilience because of how integral they are to our ability to function on a daily basis, let alone to bounce back when things don't go our way. It's a lot more difficult to overcome career and personal challenges while also juggling health challenges.

Remember also that health has a mental as well as physical component, and that mental self-care and emotional support is just as important as physical health when it comes to balancing your well-being. These days, we're lucky to live in an age in which the discourse around mental health is increasingly open and inclusive, with countless resources at our disposal to support mental and emotional wellness. Don't hesitate to find a therapist or psychiatrist who understands your individual needs and supports your personal development.

Personal growth goes hand-in-hand with professional growth, and you'll work much better if your treat yourself to a mental and physical fine-tuning!

There's something to be said for the people who not only have your back, but will go the extra mile for you every time. People who align with your values, assist in your successes, catch you when you fall, and are generally a riot to be around. They are your tribe.

- Maureen Orey

44. Find your tribe

There will always be people in your network of connections who support you, but there's something to be said for the people who not only have your back, but will go the extra mile for you every time. People who align with your values, assist in your successes, catch you when you fall, and are generally a riot to be around. They are your tribe. They are your go-to squad, your team whose support strengthens your adaptability and resilience. You can usually identify these people as those who will always be honest with you but never cruel, who will offer advice when it's constructive but understand when to step back and let you shine, who value you for the role you play in their lives and trust you to value them in turn.

Keep your tribe close and nurture those relationships, as truly exceptional allies can be few and far between Everyone deserves to have a family behind them, whether that means your blood-line, your coworkers, or your friends. Come to your tribe for advice when you're unsure about a career move. Call them up to practice the speech you're nervous about. Ask them to reach out to their networks for resources. When the time comes, you'll do the same for them.

The purpose of life is not to be happy.

It is to be useful, to be honorable, to be compassionate,

to have it make some difference that you have lived and lived well.

- Ralph Waldo Emerson

45. Be purposeful

There's difference between having a purpose and being purposeful. Being resilient is eliminating what you leave to chance. You have the power to command the space around you. Be deliberate in your words and actions, Know that all words and actions have consequences, and often that you can control whether those consequences are positive or negative. Stick to your purpose. Reflect on your vision, and every time you act, consider whether the action aligns with your values and goals. This will save you time and effort and prevent unnecessary obstacles before they arise.

Exercising purposefulness involves having a clear grasp of your values, abilities, and boundaries. Important life experiences can influence our thinking and our purpose. Yes, your purpose can change. In his book *From Murder to Forgiveness*, Azim Khasima shares about his deep personal transformation after his son was murdered. To honor his son Tariq, Azim's life's purpose shifted away from investment banking to a focus on healing the world through forgiveness when he founded the TKF Foundation an organization that helps create safer schools and communities.

We remain purposeful by staying in touch with ourselves and our goals over the course of our careers. Many people spend their whole lives trying seeking a meaningful purpose in life and work in one field because they expect their purpose to be intransigent, fixed. The reality is that purpose is largely relative, and we have the power to determine our purpose in every situation. The key to purposefulness as an ingredient to resilience is to take the time to get to know yourself and to always act deliberately and thoughtfully.

You have more power over your circumstances and your interactions with the world than you may realize. Don't let them be arbitrary.

Failing to prepare is preparing to fail.

- John Wooden

46. Prepare

A mentor used to tell me all the time, "*Preparation is the best antidote to stress.*" Over the course of my career, nothing has proven more accurate. The only consistently effective means of fighting rising levels of pressure and anxiety is preparing to tackle their sources. I've encountered few feelings as anxiety-inducing than knowing I'm under-prepared for something I care about. Fortunately, this is a pretty easy fix with a little foresight.

Use a planner, calendar or app to track your impending sources of stress for the week, month, or year, and schedule dates to prepare for them well in advance. Staying several steps ahead of the game will stop you from getting overwhelmed by the tasks ahead. If you're new to organizational tools, start out by writing daily to-do lists in your phone or notebook, and take five minutes each morning to think about what you can do that day to prepare for each item on the list. Are there things you need to buy to save yourself from scrambling for supplies later? Do you need to make plans with anyone? If you're anxious about an interaction, what questions do you want to make sure you ask or what point do you want to make sure you get across? Asking yourself even these little questions on a regular basis will keep you on top of your daily tasks and will help you stay organized and facilitate longer-term preparation.

Success requires the focus to be on the road ahead, not the route behind.

- Azim Khasima

47. Know your options

There are seldom occasions in life in which we have no control. The vast majority of the time, we have the autonomy to make our own choices, so it's only natural that the best choices are made after exploring all available options. Knowing what possibilities you have at your disposal equips you to make an informed decision about your actions, and better prepares you in case your Plan A falls through.

Sometimes it helps to get out a pen and paper and make an option map, with your available actions at the top, and the potential effects of those respective actions branching out below. Do any of your options open up new opportunities further down the road that you may want to capitalize on? Don't skimp on fleshing out your worst case-scenarios -- seeing the possible effects of our worst options often help us come to terms with their reality and reduce our anxiety by eliminating the unknown. More often than not, we realize that even the worst options are survivable if it came down to it. Laying out our options in a visual format helps us conceptualize our situation with a clearer understanding of the consequences and benefits of different actions. In so doing, we strengthen our ability to make informed and educated decisions without overlooking any potential choices or options which may prove fruitful in the future.

You are already choosing, in every moment of every day, what to give a f*ck about, so change is as simple as choosing to give a fuck about something else, It really is that simple. It's just not easy." – Mark Manson, The Subtle Art of Not Giving a F*ck

48. Choose wisely

Your choices matter.

Don't be swayed by those who don't have your best interests at heart, and don't be discouraged by naysayers. People will come in and out of your life full of advice from their own experiences and perspectives, and it will be up to you to decide how much of their input to take to heart. It's important to consider the opinions of others with humility. At the end of the day, your decisions begin and end with you. Leverage your instinct, experience, and purpose to help you make the right decisions that work for you.

There's no surer way to regret your actions than by making choices you're uncomfortable with just because someone advised you to. Your choices are yours, and you will be better equipped to handle obstacles when in situations you chose to create rather than those which you feel were thrust upon you. Remember that you have the final say in what you do with your life and the way you behave in social spaces.

Make your decision count by considering others while staying true to your values and chasing your dreams.

Forgiving yourself, believing in yourself and choosing to love yourself

are the best gifts one could receive."

- Brittany Burgunder

49. Be true to yourself

It's nearly impossible to bounce back from challenges if you're not invested in succeeding. This doesn't mean you have to put your heart and soul into causes you don't feel passionate about; rather, it means you should find missions and groups which you feel reflect your values and only apply yourself where it feels right.

Build the confidence to know your own mind and find security in your limits and goals. When you make decisions or interact with others, be sure to check in with yourself and stay true to those boundaries. Valuable individuals often get pushed into other people's ambitions for their coveted skills and assets, but only you have the power to choose which causes and missions you want to contribute to. Back to trusting your gut, if it doesn't feel right for you, it probably isn't. If you feel you're being taken advantage of or underappreciated, remember that you are your own priority and strongest advocate. It's up to you to protect yourself and speak out on your behalf.

Resilience is the ability to persist in the face of hardship. It is much more difficult to achieve success when we feel out of touch with ourself. Prioritize your values and goals and act accordingly.

It's not about finding your voice, it's about
giving yourself permission to use your voice.

- Kris Carr

50. Find your voice

When facing challenges, remember that it's important to say what you need to say. You have something unique to say, and you get to choose how to present it to the world. While it's always important to listen to others and be considerate in your discourse, don't lose your voice in the murmur of the crowd.

Everybody has a voice; it's up to each individual to find and cultivate it. Expression is a diverse and versatile tool which we all have access to and exercise differently. Those who project their voices the loudest make a conscious decision to assert a certain presence in their space, but don't be fooled -- these voices are not necessarily the most influential or powerful, they are merely the most audible. If you listen carefully, you'll notice that alongside every loud and authoritative voice is a hum of discourses, quieter inputs and advice, emails, phone calls, quips and conversations over coffee or hallway negotiations, which have as much influence over the state of affairs as the most vocal (loudest) leaders.

Explore your environment for a space in which you're comfortable voicing your opinion, be it among close colleagues, at meetings, in auditoriums, or through well-worded memos. There's no single right way to make yourself heard. The only problem is not letting yourself be heard at all. Find your voice, project it, and find confidence in being listened to.

Speaking your truth is the most powerful tool we all have.

- Oprah Winfrey

51. Speak your truth

Nobody else has had your experiences or knows your path, you are the only one who can share that particular narrative. Just as you have grown from your experiences, so other people can grow and learn from hearing them. Don't deny the world that learning opportunity. Once you've found your voice and mustered the confidence to use it, share your story. Be honest with everyone, starting with yourself.

It is said that "Perception is reality". Perspective and relativity mean that different people live and perceive different truths, and that these truths can exist symbiotically and create synergy rather than detracting from one another. Speak your truth, while acknowledging that your truth doesn't invalidate anybody else's and nobody else's truth can silence yours. The people in life who are worth listening to and support you will respect the truth you speak and help you leverage it for the greater good. Don't worry about those who don't understand; they likely have a lot of personal growth left to do before they are ready to embrace your truth. Don't wait for them. There's a whole world of people out there who are ready for your story and need to hear what you have to say.

Remain true to your vision. Remain positive. Expand and develop your perspective. Then share it, and watch it grow.

Courage is a behavior.

And like all behaviors can be developed, encouraged and reinforced.

- Bill Treasurer, *Courage Goes to Work*

52. Be courageous

Both leadership and following take courage. No matter who you are, and regardless of your work style, it takes courage to be you -- and that's okay. Nobody else is cut out to occupy your space in a community, because you are a unique contributor to the greater good. It's up to you to be courageous enough to make your contribution matter. If you're a leader, find the courage amid your humility to speak up and make the decisions that only you can make. If you're a follower, find the courage to trust your colleagues and leaders, and to advocate for yourself when necessary.

Nobody ever said this was going to be easy, but if you can bring yourself to trust yourself and your tribe to push forward and keep tackling one goal at a time, you will surprise yourself with what you can accomplish. To quote Winston Churchill:

> **"Success is not final, failure is not fatal: it is the courage to continue that counts."**
>
> *Winston Churchill*

Resilience isn't only the art of overcoming challenges; resilience is a challenge itself. It takes courage to pick yourself up, bounce back, and keep going. It takes courage to decide to try again. Find the courage to be resilient!

Made in the USA
Monee, IL
04 October 2020